Teaching Poetry
Book 2

Years 3 & 4

Louis Fidge

Published by Letts Educational
The Chiswick Centre
414 Chiswick High Road
London W4 5TF
Tel: 020 89963333
Fax: 020 87428390
email: mail@lettsed.co.uk
Website: www.letts-education.com

Letts Educational Limited is a division of Granada Learning
Limited, part of the Granada Media Group.

First published 2002

ISBN 1840856866 TEACHING POETRY BOOK 2

The author asserts the moral right to be identified as the
author of this work.

British Library Cataloguing in Publication Data
A catalogue record for this book is available from the British
Library.

This book was designed and produced for Letts Educational
by Bender Richardson White, PO Box 266, Uxbridge UB9 5NX
Commissioned by Andrew Thraves
Project management by Kate Newport
Editing by Jennifer Smart
Cover design by Mike Pilley
Book design by Ben White
Illustrations by Pamela Hewetson, Robin Lawrie,
Peter Lubach, Jo Moore, Karen Perrins, Charlotte Stowell
Production by Kerry Smith
Printed and bound in the UK by Ashford Colour Press

ACKNOWLEDGEMENTS

The publishers gratefully acknowledge the following for permission
to reproduce copyright material. Every effort has been made to
trace copyright holders, but in some cases it has proved impossible. The publishers would be happy to hear from any copyright
holder that has not been acknowledged.

'Mary and Sarah' by Richard Edwards, from *A Mouse in My Room*
published by Orchard Books. © Richard Edwards. Reprinted with
the kind permission of the author.

'The Airman' by Clive Sansom, from *Speech Rhymes* published by A
& C Black. Reprinted by permission of David Higham Associates
Limited.

'I Visited A Village' by Moses Kainwo. Reprinted with the kind permission of the author.

'Who is de Girl?' by John Agard, from *Another Day On My Feet And
I Would Have Died* published by Macmillan. Reprinted by kind permission of John Agard c/o Caroline Sheldon Literary Agency.

'Python on Piccolo' by Charles Causley from *Collected Poems for
Children* published by Macmillan. Reprinted by permission of David
Higham Associates Limited.

'Hong Kong' by Anita Marie Sackett. Reprinted by kind permission
of the author.

'Sunday in the Yarm Fard' by Trevor Millum. © Trevor Millum.
Reprinted with the kind permission of the author.

'Wordspinning' by John Foster from *Word Wizard* published by OUP
© 2001 by John Foster. Reprinted with the kind permission of the
author.

'A Spring Flower Riddle' by David Whitehead, from *Poetry
Collections* edited by Wes Magee and published by Scholastic. ©
David Whitehead. Reprinted with the kind permission of the
author.

'Two Boys Crying' by Ray Mather, from *The Scholastic Bumper Book
of Poems* edited by Wes Magee, and published by Scholastic in
1992. © Ray Mather. Reprinted with the kind permission of the
author.

'Dog Lovers' by Spike Milligan, from *Small Dreams of a Scorpion*.
Reprinted by permission of Spike Milligan Productions Limited.

'Monday's Child' by Lucy Coats from *First Rhymes* by Lucy Coats,
first published in the UK by Orchard Books in 1994, a division of
The Watts Publishing Group Limited, 96 Leonard Street, London
EC2A 4XD. Reprinted with permission of the publishers.

'I Want to Be An Astronaut' by Peter Thabit Jones from *Scholastic
Collections: Poetry* compiled by Wes Magee and published by
Scholastic. © Peter Thabit Jones. Reprinted with the kind permis-
sion of the author.

'The Digger's Song' by John Foster from *Four O'Clock Friday* published by OUP. © 1991 John Foster. Reprinted with the kind permission of the author.

'Toboggan' by David Whitehead, from *Secrets* edited by Judith
Nicholls and published by Ginn in 1998. © David Whitehead.
Reprinted with the kind permission of the author.

'The Magic Box' by Kit Wright, from *Cat Among the Pigeons* by Kit
Wright, (Viking Kestrel, 1987) Copyright © Kit Wright, 1984, 1987.
Reprinted by permission of Penguin Books Limited.

Contents

What is Colour Like?

Before you begin

What are some of the problems of not being able to see?
What would you miss most if you could not see?

What is Colour Like?

I asked the boy who cannot see,
"What is colour like?"
"Green," said he,
"Is like the sound of leaves
When the wind blows through
The forest;
Running water is blue;
And red, I think,
Is like the sound of a trumpet;
The smell of roses is pink;
Purple is like a thunderstorm,
Yellow is something
Soft and warm;
White is the quietness when you lie
And dream."

Anon.

Reading

1. How did the boy describe his idea of the colour green?

2. What colour did running water remind him of?

3. What did he think red was like?

4. What did he think purple was like?

5. How did the boy describe yellow?

6. Use copymaster 1 to read two more poems about colour.
    Which poem do you think describes colours best? Say why.

Writing

1. Think of a colour and list as many things as possible of that colour.
    Describe each thing in an interesting way.
    Choose five of your best descriptions.
    Write them out as a list.
    They do not have to rhyme. Do it like this:

    > *Red*
    > *The last glimpse of the sun as it sets.*
    > *My face after running as fast as I can.*
    > *The drop of blood on my skin when the rose thorn pricked me.*
    > *A traffic light commanding cars to stop.*
    > *My nose in the cold weather!*

2. Write down the colours you associate with different feelings, like this:

    > *Fear is white. Envy is green.*

3. The boy in the poem said what each colour made him think of.
    Choose a colour and do the same and write a short poem.
    It does not have to rhyme. Do it like this:

    > *Yellow*
    > *Yellow is soft and warm.*
    > *It is a sandy beach.*
    > *It is a bowl of cornflakes with cold milk.*
    > *It brings happiness and light.*
    > *Yellow is licking a lollipop in summer.*

The Airman

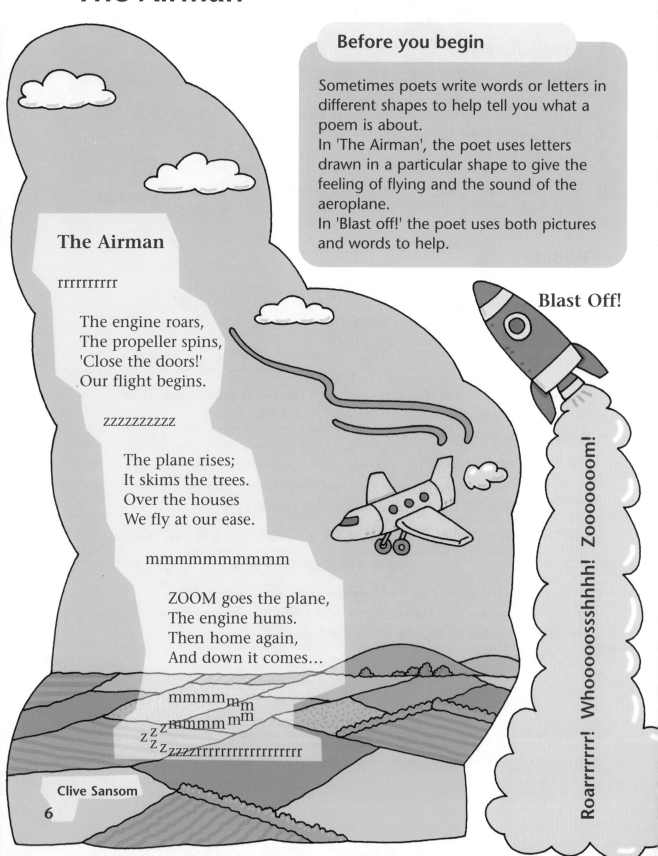

Before you begin

Sometimes poets write words or letters in different shapes to help tell you what a poem is about.

In 'The Airman', the poet uses letters drawn in a particular shape to give the feeling of flying and the sound of the aeroplane.

In 'Blast off!' the poet uses both pictures and words to help.

Blast Off!

The Airman

rrrrrrrrrr

The engine roars,
The propeller spins,
'Close the doors!'
Our flight begins.

zzzzzzzzzz

The plane rises;
It skims the trees.
Over the houses
We fly at our ease.

mmmmmmmmmm

ZOOM goes the plane,
The engine hums.
Then home again,
And down it comes…

mmmm m m
mmmm m m
z z z
z z zzzzrrrrrrrrrrrrrrrrrrrrr

Clive Sansom

Roarrrrrr! Whoooossshhhh! Zoooooom!

6

Reading

1. What is 'The Airman' all about?

2. What three letters does the poet use to give the sound of the aeroplane?

3. Why are the letters at the end of the poem written in a particular shape?

4. What is 'Blast Off!' all about?

5. Which words are used in 'Blast Off!'? (Write them correctly spelt!)

6. Why do you think the words in 'Blast Off!' are spelt in the way they are?

Writing

1. Sometimes we can make a shape poem with just one letter! Look at this poem about a queue at a bus stop.

Use pictures and just the letter given to represent these subjects below. Experiment with your ideas in rough, first. Make a best copy in your book when you are happy.

   a) a swarm of bees (B)   b) a cup (or pot) of tea (T)
   c) a rough sea (C)   d) someone humming a tune (m)
   e) a mosquito buzzing (Z)   f) a snake hissing (s)

2. Sometimes we can write words in interesting ways to make people think of their meanings. These are called calligrams. For example:

$$\text{j}^{\frown}\text{m}^{\frown}\text{u}^{\frown}\text{p}^{\frown}\text{i}^{\frown}\text{n}^{\frown}\text{g}$$

Choose four of these words and make calligrams of them.
Experiment with your ideas in rough, first. Make a best copy in your book when you are happy.

   TRIP   LEAP   POP   SHIVER   PULL   PUSH

   TALL   FAT   SPLASH   FIRE   RAIN   BIRD

3. See copymaster 2 for some further examples of calligrams.

Mary and Sarah

Before you begin

What things are smooth and soft to touch?
What things are rough and hard to touch?

Mary and Sarah

Mary likes smooth things,
Things that glide:
Sleek skis swishing
Down a mountainside.

Mary likes smooth things,
Things all mellow:
Milk, silk, runny honey,
Tunes on a cello.

Mary says – polish,
Sarah says – rust,
Mary says mayonnaise,
Sarah says – crust.

Give me, says Mary,
The slide of a stream,
The touch of a petal,
A bowl of ice cream.

Sarah likes rough things,
Things that snatch:
Boats with barnacled bottoms,
Thatch.

Sarah likes rough things,
Things all troubly:
Crags, snags, bristles, thistles,
Fields left stubbly.

Sarah says – hedgehogs,
Mary says – seals,
Sarah says – sticklebacks,
Mary says – eels.

Give me, says Sarah,
The gales of a coast,
The husk of a chestnut,
A plate of burnt toast.

Mary and Sarah –
They'll never agree
Till peaches and coconuts
Grow on one tree.

Richard Edwards

Reading

1. What sort of things does: a) Mary like? b) Sarah like?

2. Write down three things: a) Mary likes b) Sarah likes

3. What do you think the last verse means?

4. Find and write down five pairs of rhyming words from the poem.

5. How many verses does the poem have?

6. Do you agree that it would be very boring if everyone liked the same things?

Writing

1. Make a list of hot and cold things, like this:

hot things	cold things
a pizza straight from the oven	*an ice cube on the tongue*

2. We use our hands for touching and feeling.
   Copy and complete these two verses about hands.
   Make up two more verses of your own.

Hands can touch.	*Hands can feel.*
Hands can mend.	*Hands can _____.*
Hands can hug	*Hands can show*
Your best _____.	*How much you care.*

3. 'Mary and Sarah' is all about opposites.
   List some of the things you like and hate.
   Turn your ideas into a poem. (It does not have to rhyme.)
   Write several verses, each with three lines.
   Here is the start of one child's poem to give you the idea:

I like smiling	*I hate spiders*
and hugging and chatting.	*and dogs that bark and snarl.*
These are some things that I like.	*These are some things that I hate.*

4. Use copymaster 3 to help you write a poem called 'I Would Rather…'

The Octopus

Before you begin

A 'shape' poem is a list of words thoughts or ideas which are presented in a particular way or shape to remind you of the subject in some way. Which shape poem below do you like the best?

old rusty car
dirty and dented
broken and bent
flat tyres

windows broken
engine oily
starts with a bang
throws out clouds of

cough! splutter! choke!
nasty, black, evil smoke!

licky
sticky
drippy
slippy
icy
nicy
lollipop

I'm Ollie the Octopus
I live on the sea bed
I've got a slimy body
And eight long legs.
I'm greeny brown
And hard to see.
I eat little fishes
For my tea!

nose.
my
follow
and
going
just keep
goes. I'll
see where it
this path and
I'll just follow

I'm a bouncing rubber ball. I bounce along and hit the wall. That's all!

Reading

1. a) Which poem is about a path?
    b) Why do you think the words get smaller at the end of the poem?

2. a) Which poem is a long thin poem?   b) Which words rhyme in it?

3. Why do you think the poem about the car finishes in the way it does?

4. Why do you think there are eight lines in the poem about the octopus?

5. Why does the rubber ball stop bouncing?

6. Which poem did you like best? Say why.

Writing

1. Use the outline pictures on copymaster 4 to help you
    plan some shape poems about:

    a snail   a spider   a ladder

    - Write some interesting words inside each shape about
      that particular subject.
    - The words may rhyme, but they do not have to.
    - If you wish, you can compose some simple
      rhyming sentences instead.
    - Experiment with your ideas. Change anything you wish.
    - When you are happy, make a best copy.

2. Choose some of the subjects below.
    Make up simple shape poems about them, like the ones opposite.

    stairs   a hedgehog   mountains   string   fireworks

    - Write an interesting sentence or set of sentences
      about the subject in rough.
    - Experiment with your ideas and turn them into a shape poem.
    - When you are happy with your ideas, make a best copy in your book.

3. Make up a shape poem about a subject of your own choice.

Windy Nights

Before you begin

Think of as many words describing the sound of the wind as possible. Here are a few to start you off: *The wind howls and sighs and whistles and roars.*

Windy Nights

Rumbling in the chimneys,
Rattling at the doors,
Round the roofs and round the roads
The rude wind roars;
Raging through the darkness,
Raving through the trees,
Racing off again across
The great grey seas.

Rodney Bennett

Reading

1. What does the wind do in the chimneys?

2. What sound does the wind make round the roofs and roads?

3. Do the words 'raging' and 'raving' tell you the wind is gentle or rough?

4. Where does the wind race off to?

5. a) What do you notice about lots of words in the poem?
   b) Why do you think the poet has written the poem in this way?

6. Read the poem on copymaster 5. In what ways is it similar to the poem in this unit? Which do you prefer? Why?

Writing

1. What does the noise of the wind at night remind you of?
   Read this poem and write one of your own, like it.

   > The wind at night is like a wild cat screeching.
   > The wind at night is like someone moaning in pain.
   > The wind at night is like a giant sighing.
   > The wind at night is like the swish of a skirt.
   > The wind is. The wind is.

2. Make a list of nice and nasty noises you hear at night.

Nice noises at night	Nasty noises at night
the muted sound of the TV	water gurgling strangely in pipes

3. Copy and complete this poem about things you might hear in bed at night.

   > Footsteps on stairs, people moving chairs,
   > Floorboards creaking, mouse _____,
   > Toilet flushing, cars _____,
   > Wind in the trees, a loud _____,
   > Telephone ringing, sound of _____,
   > _____
   > _____
   > Then mysteriously, it seems, sounds become dreams!

I Visited a Village

Before you begin

How do you feel when you have tried hard and done something really well?
Does it make you happy?
Discuss how you could perform this poem as a group.
Would you include any actions or sounds?

I Visited a Village

I visited a village
And the dancers were dancing.
They danced with all their hearts
And my whole life smiled.

I visited a school
And the teachers were teaching.
They taught with all their hearts
And my whole life smiled.

I visited a clinic
And the nurses were nursing.
They nursed with all their hearts
And my whole life smiled.

I visited a farm
And the farmers were farming.
They farmed with all their hearts
And my whole life smiled.

I came back home
And my parents were waving.
They waved with all their hearts
And my whole life smiled.

Moses Kainwo

Reading

1. a) What is the title of the poem?   b) Who wrote it?

2. a) How many verses are there?
   b) How many lines are there in each verse?

3. What do you notice about the last line of each verse?

4. Is it a rhyming poem? Do you think this matters?

5. List the places the poet visited, in order.

6. What do you think this old proverb means? 'If you want to be happy
   you must have something to do, something or someone to love and
   something to hope for.'

Writing

1. Copy and complete this extra verse for the poem.

   I visited a football match.
   All the people were playing.
   They _____ with all their hearts
   And _____ .

2. Make up some more verses for the poem. Write about when you visit:

   a hospital and see some doctors
   a building site and see some builders
   a circus and see some jugglers

3. Think of some other places you could visit and make up your own verses.

4. Use copymaster 6 to help you write another performance poem, called
   'The Sea Goes on For Ever'.

Python on Piccolo

Before you begin

How many different musical instruments can you name?
Discuss how you could perform the poem below.
Could you include any sound effects?

Python on Piccolo

Python on piccolo
Dingo on drums,
Gannet on gee-tar
Sits and strums.

Croc on cornet
Goes to town,
Sloth on sitar
Upside-down.

Toad on tuba
Sweet and strong,
Crane on clarinet,
Goat on gong.
And the sun jumped up in the morning.

Toucan travelling
On trombone,
Zebra zapping
On xylophone.

Beaver on bugle
Late and soon,
Boa constrictor
On bassoon.

Tiger on trumpet
Blows up a storm,
Flying fox
On flügelhorn.
And the sun jumped up in the morning.

Extract from a poem by Charles Causley

Reading

1. Which instrument does each of these animals play:
   a) python?   b) sloth?   c) tiger?   d) zebra?   e) goat?

2. Which animal plays:
   a) cornet?   b) bugle?   c) clarinet?   d) tuba?   e) flugelhorn?

3. a) What is the title of the poem?   b) Who wrote it?

4. The same line appears twice in the poem. What is it?

5. Which word in the poem rhymes with:
   a) drums?   b) town?   c) strong?   d) trombone?   e) soon?

6. Say something you liked about the poem.

Writing

1. Copy and complete these extra verses in your own words.

   Polar bear on banjo
   Flamingo on flute,
   Vulture plays the violin
   Wearing a _____.

   Snake shakes a tambourine
   Rabbit rings a bell,
   The _____ plays the double bass
   Ever so _____.

   Penguin plays piano
   The _____ is on saxophone,
   The fawn with the French horn
   Wants to be left all _____.
   And the sun _____ up in the _____.

2. Work with a partner.
   Make up a performance poem of your own about the patterns of a normal day.
   Copy the verses below and make up some more of your own.
   Decide how you will read your poem aloud to others.
   Will you also act it out?

   The sun arises.   *The sun gets hot.*   *The sun fills the sky.*
   Yes, the sun arises.   *Yes, the sun gets hot.*   *Yes, the sun fills the sky.*

3. Use copymaster 7 to help you write your own poem to perform, called 'Ants Like Acting'.

Who is de Girl?

Before you begin

Some poems are good for reading aloud and for performing as a group.
Discuss how you might perform this poem.
How can you tell that the poem below is written by a Caribbean poet?

Who is de Girl?

who is de girl dat kick de ball
then jump for it over de wall

sallyann is a girl so full-o zest
sallyann is a girl dat just can't rest

who is de girl dat pull de hair
of de bully and make him scare

sallyann is a girl so full-o zest
sallyann is a girl dat just can't rest

who is de girl dat bruise she knee
when she fall from de mango tree

sallyann is a girl so full-o zest
sallyann is a girl dat just can't rest

who is de girl dat set de pace
when boys and girls dem start to race

sallyann is a girl so full-o zest
sallyann is a girl dat just can't rest

John Agard

Reading

1. Who is the poem about?

2. What sort of girl do you think she is?

3. Write down the words of the chorus
   (the verse that is repeated several times).

4. Write down a word from the poem that rhymes with:
   a) zest   b) ball   c) hair   d) knee   e) pace

5. What do you notice about the way the poem is written?

6. Do you think this is a good poem to perform? Say why.

Writing

1. Rewrite two of the verses and choruses. Change the name
   of Sallyann to a boy's name.

2. Write another verse for the poem about Sallyann in your own words.

3. Rewrite the poem in standard English as you might say it.
   Include punctuation, like this:

   > *Who is the girl that kicks the ball,*
   > *Then jumps for it over the wall?*

4. Work with a partner.
   Write a performance poem to help you learn your tables.
   Pick a times table you need to learn.
   Here is the beginning of a times table poem to give you an idea:

Once two is two.	*Two two's are four.*
Violets are white and blue.	*Someone's knocking at the door.*

   Work with a group and discuss how you might perform your poem to
   others.

5. Use copymaster 8 to help you write another poem to perform.

Hong Kong

Before you begin

What do you know about Hong Kong?
Read the poem below and find out!
Discuss how you could read the poem in an interesting way as a class.

Hong Kong

High rise flats,
Jumbo jets,
Sampan village,
Fishing nets.

Sleek trains,
Antique trams,
Island ferries,
Traffic jams.

Busy markets,
Bamboo shoots,
Caged song birds,
Ginger roots.

Fried rice,
Charcoal pot,
Dried squid,
Chilli hot.

Pungent smells,
Crowded street,
Lion dances,
Drumming beat.

Bronze Buddha,
Wind chimes,
Designer shops,
Neon signs.

City banks,
Discos, bars,
Travellers' cheques,
Credit cards.

Jade, silk,
Suits, tea,
Cameras, watches,
Duty free.

Chinese scrolls,
Lacquered bold,
Lucky packets,*
Red and gold.

Fragrant Harbour,
Mango moon,
Festive fireworks,
On Kowloon.

Peach blossom,
Twinkling lights,
Kumquat trees,
Cooler nights.

Orange lanterns,
Temple gong,
Lunar New Year,
In Hong Kong.

Anita Marie Sackett

* Lucky packets (*Li shi*) are given at New Year to wish good luck, good health and prosperity.

Reading

1. a) What is the poem called?   b) Who wrote it?

2. a) How many verses are there in the poem?
   b) Does the poem rhyme?

3. a) How many lines are there in each verse?
   b) Are the lines long or short? Why do you think this is?

4. Write down five interesting words from the poem and what they mean.
   (Use a dictionary to help you if necessary.)

5. Did you like the poem? Give a reason for your answer.

Writing

1. Copy and complete this poem about a birthday celebration.

   Birthday cards,
   Presents, too,
   Party begins
   At half past _____.

   Fizzy drinks,
   Sausages on _____,
   Conjuror comes
   To _____ some tricks.

   Loud music,
   _____ of noise,
   Happy _____,
   Happy boys.

   Excited children
   In fancy dress,
   Party's over –
   What a _____!

2. Work with a partner.
   Make up a performance poem like 'Hong Kong'
   about the place where you live.
   Decide how you will read your poem aloud to others.
   Here is an idea to get you started:

   There are people with shopping bags
   And people driving cars,
   Some children are playing,
   Some are eating chocolate bars.

3. Use copymaster 9 to help you write a performance poem called 'My
   Day at School'.

Forest Sounds

Before you begin

What sort of noises do you think you might hear in a forest?
Discuss how you could perform the poem below as a group.
Try to make the sounds as realistic as possible.

Forest Sounds

We are the trees in the forest.
Swish-a-whisper-swish.

*And we are the winds that
Blow and sigh, blow and sigh.*

We are the streams in the forest that
Gurgle and tinkle, gurgle and tinkle.

*And we are the winds that
Blow and sigh, blow and sigh.*

We are the fish in the river that
Splash, tumble, splash; splash, tumble, splash.

*And we are the winds that
Blow and sigh, blow and sigh.*

We are the thunder clouds that
Boom-a-boom, boom; boom-a-boom, boom.

*And we are the winds that
Blow and sigh, blow and sigh.*

Reading

1. Where is the poem set (where does it take place)?

2. What is the poem all about?

3. List five things you would hear in the forest.

4. What noise do these make:
   a) the winds?   b) the streams?   c) the thunder clouds?

5. Explain what a chorus is.

6. Practise reading 'What Some People Do' on copymaster 10 with a partner or a small group and, when you are ready, perform it to others.

Writing

1. Copy and complete the beginning of this poem called 'Seaside Sounds'.

   Verse 1   *We are the seagulls that*
   Soar and shriek, soar and _____.

   Chorus   *We are the waves that*
   Crash and splash, _____ and splash.

   Verse 2   *We are the pebbles that*
   Rattle and clatter, _____.

   Chorus   _____
   _____

2. Now make up some more verses of your own about the sounds of these:

   ships   winds   children   fish

   (Don't forget the chorus after each verse!)
   Practise reading your poem aloud with a partner or small group.

3. Copy and complete this verse about noises people and animals make.
   Make up two more verses of your own and practise reading them aloud.

   Lions roar, parrots squawk,
   Elephants trumpet, people _____.

Funny People

Before you begin

Do you have a good sense of humour?
What sort of things make you laugh?
Some poems are intended just to make us smile.

As I Was Walking Down the Street

As I was walking down the street
I met a man called Fred.
Boing! Boing! Boing! Boing!
Fred loved bouncing on his head.

As I was walking down the street
I met a lady called Ann.
Ann was always washing her face
In a greasy frying pan.

Deborah Delora

Deborah Delora she liked a bit of fun.
She went to the baker's and she bought a bun.
Dipped the bun in honey and threw it at her mother.
Then she got another and threw it at her brother!

My Teacher

Teacher, teacher, suck your thumb,
Blow a bubble with some gum.
Teacher, teacher, I don't care,
Make a face and pull your hair.
Teacher, teacher, scream and shout.
Open my cage and let me out!

Reading

1. a) What did Fred like to do?   b) Where did Ann wash her face?

2. What did Deborah Delora do for fun?

3. Who is the last poem about?

4. What do you think makes each of the poems funny?

5. Which poem did you like best? Say why.

6. Read and compare the humorous 'bird' poems on copymaster 11.

Writing

1. Make up a funny second line for each of these:

   a) *My great Auntie Jane*

   _____

   b) *Last year I saw a polar bear*

   _____

   c) *I have a friend called Caroline*

   _____

   d) *Billy, Billy, suck your toe*

   _____

2. Now think of a funny way to complete this rhyme.

   > *As I was walking down the street,*
   > *I met a boy called _____.*

   _____

   _____

3. Make up some more silly verses for the 'My Teacher' poem.

4. Make up another verse about Deborah Delora.

5. Copy and finish off these verses in your own way.

   a) *It was a summer's day in winter*
      And snow was raining fast,

   _____

   _____

   b) *One fine October morning*
      In September, last July,

   _____

   _____

Punnier and Punnier

Before you begin

Do you know why the man put some toadstools on top of the fridge?
Because there wasn't mushroom inside!
Jokes, like the one above, often use puns. (A pun is the deliberate use of words with similar sounds to create a humorous effect. In the joke, 'mushroom' = 'much room')
Do you know any good jokes that play with words?

Punny Books

Have you ever read …
'Jumping Off Cliffs' by Hugo First
'Mountain Rescues' by Justin Time
'The Sky at Night' by I.C. Stars
'Chinese Astronauts' by Fly Ying
'Helping with the Housework' by Y. Mee
'The Unsolved Mystery' by W.H.O Dunnett
'The Nameless Rodent' by Anony Mouse
'The Bandit' by Robin Banks

Rhyming Riddles

What do you call …

… a conceited horse-rider?	A cocky jockey.
… a joyful race?	A fun run.
… a young hen that is ill?	A sick chick.
… a fizzy drink store?	A pop shop.
… a buzzing insect that has escaped?	A free bee.
… an angry employer?	A cross boss.
… a plate of sea food?	A fish dish.
… an overweight rodent?	A fat rat.

Am I an overweight rodent or a fat rat?

Reading

1. What is a pun?

2. Who wrote:
    a) Mountain Rescues?   b) The Sky at Night?
    c) Chinese Astronauts?   d) The Nameless Rodent?

3. Write the name of each author in a different way.
    Do it like this: Hugo First = You go first

4. Which author's name did you think was the cleverest pun?

5. What do you notice about the answers to all the riddles?

6. Which answer did you think was the funniest?

Writing

1. Match up these book titles with their authors. Write them in your book.

How To Be an Entertainer	M. T. Bag
The Fire in the Cathedral	I. B. Bare
The Art of Pickpocketing	R. U. Joking
Observing Carefully	G. E. Tabus
Nudism	C. Here
Public Transport	Ho Lee Smoke

2. Make up a good book title for each of these authors:

    a) B. A. Dear   b) G. Gee   c) I. O. U. A. Pound

3. Copy and complete these rhyming riddles

Not long before midday	s _ _n n _ _ n
High speed aeroplane collection	j _ _ s _ _
Extremely jolly	v _ _ _ m _ _ _ _
Single pebble	l _ _ _ st _ _ _
Fresh evidence	n _ _ cl _ _

4. Here are some answers to some more rhyming riddles.
    Make up a clue for each.
    a) spare chair   b) wet vet   c) night light   d) bad lad   e) not hot

5. Work out the answers to the 'Knock, knock!' jokes on copymaster 12.

Sunday in the Yarm Fard

Before you begin

Do you like chish and fips or mangers and bash?
What makes the names of the food above funny?
Read the poem below in which the poet has deliberately played about with
words in a similar way to create a humorous effect.

Sunday in the Yarm Fard

The mat keowed
The mow cooed
The bog darked
The kigeon pooed

The squicken chalked
The surds bang
The kwuck dacked
The burch rells chang

And then, after all the dacking and changing
The chalking and banging
The darking and pooing
The keowing and kooing
There was a mewtiful beaumont
Of queace and pie-ate.

Trevor Millum

Reading

1. a) What is the poem called?   b) Who wrote it?

2. What:

   a) keowed?   b) cooed?   c) darked?

3. Why do you think the poet has mixed up the beginnings of some words?

4. Write the first verse with all the words correctly spelt.

5. Do you prefer the correctly spelt verse or the verse as it is in the poem? Give a reason for your answer.

6. Did you like the poem? Say why (or why not).

Writing

1. Mix up the beginning and ending of these words.
   The first is done for you.

   a) bucket and spade = spucket and bade   b) salt and pepper
   c) horse and cart   d) cup and saucer
   e) girls and boys   f) men and women

2. Copy the beginning of this shopping list of 'unusual items'.
   Add ten more of your own.

   > *a lottle of bemonade*
   > *a broaf of lead*
   > *a backet of piscuits*

3. Here is the beginning of a well-known traditional story.
   Can you work out what it is?
   Write a few more sentences of the story in a similar way.

   One day a mittle old lan and a wittle old loman made a bingerbread goy.
   They hopped pim into the oven to cook.

4. Use copymaster 13 to help you write a funny poem of your own, like the one opposite.

A Spring Flower Riddle

Before you begin

A riddle is a kind of secret puzzle.
You are given some clues and you have to try to work out the answer.
Do you know any riddles?
Can you solve the riddles in the poem? Use the pictures to help you!

A Spring Flower Riddle

1. As our simple wintry name implies –
   A fall of crystal whiteness from the skies.

2. Our golden trumpets shout loud and strong –
   Winter's gone! Spring won't be long!

3. Tiny goblets of yellow, mauve and blue –
   These little cups collect the morning dew.

4. On grassy banks our prim, creamy flowers
   Bring a burst of colour after April's showers.

5. Million upon million tiny fairy bells
   Make a bright blues carpet in the woodland dells.

6. I grow by the roadside, sun-yellow flowers.
   When my petals are gone I blow away the hours.

7. Tiny white stars chain-stitched across the lawn.
   Called the day's eye; wide-eyed from early dawn.

8. I hide in the woodland, shy and tiny by the hedge.
   Sweet-scented - I'm a colour at the rainbow's edge.

9. Put together we make a Spring Bouquet –
   But where we live is where we love to stay.

David Whitehead

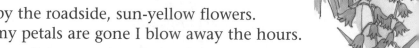

Answers: 1. Snowdrops 2. Daffodils 3. Crocuses 4. Primroses 5. Bluebells 6. Dandelions 7. Daisies 8. Violets

Reading

1. Explain what a riddle is.

2. a) What is the poem called? b) Who wrote it?

3. List the names of the spring flowers that begin with 'd'.

4. How do the pictures help you?

5. What do you think the last verse means?

6. Read and work out some more riddles on copymaster 14.

Writing

1. Copy these riddles. Choose the correct answer for each from the box.

> balloon   chair   key   television

> a) I have four legs but cannot walk.
>   I carry your weight when you take the weight off your feet.
>
> b) I have one eye. You can see me but I can't see you!
>   Switch me on and I come to life!
>
> c) I have a skin just like you. I am light as the air.
>   You are not kind to me. You blow me up and hit me.
>
> d) I am hard. You give me a ring. I let you in.

2. Follow the rules below and make up some riddles for the following things.

   a table   a car   an elephant   an aeroplane   a mirror

> Rules for riddlers!
>
> • Pretend you are the thing you are writing about.
> • Describe it accurately without saying what the thing is.
> • Try to make the thing sound a little strange or confusing.
> • Give enough clues but don't say too much,
>   or you will make it too easy!

Wordspinning

Before you begin

An anagram is when you change the letters around in a word to make another word. For example, 'meat' becomes 'team' and 'salt' becomes 'last'. Read the poem below in which the poet has cleverly used anagrams to create a humorous effect.

Wordspinning

Spin pins into nips.
Snap pans into naps.
Mix spit into tips.
Turn parts into traps.

Switch post into stop.
Whisk dare into dear.
Carve hops into shop.
Rip rate into tear.

Twist tame into mate.
Make mean into name.
Juggle taste into state.
In the wordspinning game.

John Foster

Reading

1. What is an anagram?

2. a) What is the title of the poem?   b) Who wrote it?

3. Write an anagram for:
   a) pins   b) post   c) tame   d) taste   e) hops   f) rate

4. What do you think 'wordspinning' means?

5. Do you think this is a clever poem? Explain your answer.

Writing

1. Make anagrams of the words below. The first has been done for you.

   a) nerve – never b) part   c) lump   d) act   e) eat
   f) bowl   g) read   h) felt   i) charm   j) cares

2. Write each of these words backwards and make some new words.

   a) ten   b) pin   c) mug   d) tip   e) saw
   f) rats   g) spot   h) flow   i) flog   j) evil

3. Write each of these words backwards. What do you notice about them?

   a) deed   b) pop   c) eye   d) level   e) peep
   f) noon   g) madam   h) rotor   i) solos   j) mum

4. Notice that the first and last letters of the underlined words have been
   changed around. Copy the poem and complete the missing words.

   > Make <u>loop</u> into <u>pool</u>, turn <u>loot</u> into <u>tool</u>.
   > Spin <u>pin</u> into <u>nip</u>, change <u>pit</u> into _____.
   > Make <u>leap</u> into <u>peal</u>, turn <u>lead</u> into _____.
   > Spin <u>top</u> into <u>pot</u>, change <u>ton</u> into _____.
   > Make <u>dam</u> into <u>mad</u>, turn <u>dab</u> into _____.
   > Spin <u>nap</u> into <u>pan</u>, change <u>nab</u> into _____.

5. Use copymaster 15 to help you write a poem called 'Weekdays,
   Weakdays', which plays with the names of the days of the week.

Two Boys Crying

Have you ever been disappointed because you could not have something you wanted really badly?

Two Boys Crying

Across the world
Two boys are crying,
Both wanting more
And tired of trying.

The first boy wants a mountain bike
And blames his Mum for being mean;
Had enough of the daily hike,
He's desperate to be part of the scene.
All day long
The wanting burns strong.
All the night
The wanting burns bright.
So little to ask,
Bikes are everywhere;
Oh, why is life so unfair?

The second boy wants something to eat
But is too weak to place the blame.
His mother weeps, helpless, dead-beat,
While his father hangs his head in shame.
All day long
The wanting burns strong.
All the night
The wanting burns bright.
So little to ask,
Food is everywhere;
Oh, why is life so unfair?

Across the world
Two boys are crying,
Both wanting more
And tired of trying.

Ray Mather

Reading

1. The poem begins and ends with the same chorus that tells us what the poem is all about. Copy the chorus in your book.

2. a) What does the first boy want?   b) Why does he want it?

3. Who does the boy blame for not giving him a bike?

4. a) What does the second boy want?   b) Why does he want it?

5. a) Why do you think his mother weeps?
   b) Why do you think his father feels ashamed?

6. The poem is meant to make us think.
   What can we learn from the poem?

7. Read the poem called 'Pollution' on copymaster 16.

Writing

1. Rewrite the two verses of the poem. Put yourself in the place of the two boys. Do it like this:

   I want a mountain bike
   I blame my Mum for being mean;

2. Imagine it is your birthday tomorrow.
   Write a poem contrasting two different points of view in your book.
   a) On the left-hand page write a list of five things you would really like.
   Your list does not have to rhyme. Begin by writing this chorus first.

   Dear _____,
   It's a special day – it's my birthday tomorrow.
   And birthdays are days for joy not sorrow.
   I've listed some things I would really like below.
   Let me have one of them – and see me glow!

   b) Now imagine you were a very poor child. Your needs would be very different. On the right-hand page write the same chorus at the beginning. Underneath write a list of five things you would really like.
   c) Think of a good title. Illustrate the two parts of your poem in an appropriate way.

Dog Lovers

Before you begin

Do you have a pet dog?
Discuss some of the good things about having a dog.
Discuss some of the disadvantages.

Dog Lovers

So they bought you
And kept you in a
Very good home
Central heating
TV
A deep freeze
A very good home –
No one to take you
For that lovely long run –
But otherwise
'A very good home.'
They fed you on Pal and Chum
But not that lovely long run,
Until, mad with energy and boredom
You escaped – and ran and ran and ran
Under a car.
Today they will cry for you –
Tomorrow they will buy another dog.

Spike Milligan (1918-2002)

Reading

1. How can you tell the people who bought the dog were well-off?

2. In what ways did the people give the dog what it needed?

3. In what ways did the people not look after the dog properly?

4. Why do you think the dog ran away?

5. What happened to the dog?

6. What do you think we can learn from the poem?

Writing

1. What sort of things do dogs like? What do they hate?
   Copy the sentences below. Write some more of your own,
   as if you were a dog. Begin each sentence on a new line.

   I love going for walks but I hate it when it thunders.
   I love shaking myself when I'm wet but I hate staying at home alone.

2. What do dogs make you think of in different situations?
   Copy and finish these sentences in interesting ways.

   When a dog chases a cat it looks like a rocket roaring along.
   When a dog curls up in its basket it looks like _____.
   When a dog comes out of the sea it looks like _____.
   When a dog jumps up to catch a ball it looks like _____.
   When a dog wags its tail it looks like _____.
   When a dog growls angrily it looks like _____.

3. Imagine you are a dog. What do different parts of your body feel like
   e.g. your nose, your claws, your ears, your tail, your fur, your whiskers?
   Write a sentence about each, like this:

   My nose is like a damp sponge.
   My claws are as sharp as knives.

4. Use copymaster 17 for making up your own poem about a dog.
   Compare your poem with the poem opposite.

Monday's Child

Before you begin

Read and compare the two poems below.
Which one do you like best? Why?

Monday's Child

Monday's child is fair of face,
Tuesday's child is full of grace.
Wednesday's child is full of woe,
Thursday's child has far to go.
Friday's child is loving and giving,
Saturday's child works hard for a living.
But the child that is born on the Sabbath day,
Is bonny and blithe and good always.

Traditional

Monday's child chews kippered plaice,
Tuesday's child has an eggy face.
Wednesday's child is full of toast,
Thursday's child can eat the most.
Friday's child has the biggest tum,
Saturday's child throws beans at his mum.
But the child who is born on the Sabbath Day
Has sunlight for breakfast, with buttered sea-spray.

Lucy Coats

Reading

1. In the first poem which child:
   a) is full of grace?   b) is full of woe?   c) works hard?

2. What do you think these words mean:
   a) grace?   b) woe?   c) Sabbath day?   d) bonny?

3. In the second poem which child:
   a) has an eggy face?   b) eats the most?   c) has the biggest tum?

4. What do you think the last line of the second poem means?

5. Which poem is the traditional rhyme?
   Which one do you think is a modern version? Explain your answer.

6. Which poem did you prefer? Say why.

Writing

1. Copy and complete this poem in your own words.

   > Monday's child likes eating chips,
   > Tuesday's child has _____.
   > Wednesday's child has a spotty face,
   > Thursday's child _____.
   > Friday's child snores in bed,
   > Saturday's child _____.
   > But the child who is born on the Sabbath Day
   > _____.

2. Now make up your own version of the poem.

3. Finish off these versions of traditional rhymes in your own words:

   > Humpty Dumpty fell out of bed.
   > Humpty Dumpty bumped his head.
   > He broke his leg
   > And cracked his shell
   > _____!

   > Little Harry Horner
   > Hid around the corner
   > Waiting to jump on his friend.
   > _____
   > _____
   > _____

4. Use copymaster 18. Write a modern version of 'Solomon Grundy'.

Anger

Before you begin

What makes you angry?
How do you feel inside when you are angry?
What sort of things do you do?

Anger

I was angry. I was mad.
I seemed to have hot water bubbling inside me,
And as I got madder and madder,
I got hotter and hotter under the collar.
I was in a rage.
Colours began to flash in my head,
Oranges, yellow, black and red.
As I got madder and madder.
My eyes began to bulge.
They swivelled up and down,
Round and round.
It was frightening.
It was horrible.
My anger would not go away.
I had no control over it.
I was boiling with anger.
I was steaming with anger.
I clenched my fists.
I ground my teeth.
I stamped my foot.
I slammed the door.
Then it was gone,
Anger – horrible, black, madness.

Reading

1. What do you think made the poet angry?

2. What did the poet say he seemed to have inside him?

3. What colours does the poet use to describe anger?

4. List some things the poet did when he was angry.

5. Does the poem rhyme? Does it matter?

6. How well do you think the poet describes anger? Explain your answer.

Writing

1. Look up 'angry' in a thesaurus.
   Write down other words with a similar meaning.

2. Think about when you are angry.
   Make some lists of the following things:

   a) What you feel like.   b) How you look.

   c) What you think about.   d) What sort of things you do.

3. Choose some of your best ideas and turn them into a poem.
   It does not have to rhyme.
   Start each new thought on a new line.
   Illustrate your poem when you have finished it.
   Begin like this:

   When I was angry …

4. Use copymaster 19 to make a 'map of your feelings' and what
   each feeling makes you think of. Use this as a starting point for writing
   other poems about different feelings.

In Summer When I Go to Bed

Before you begin

If you could be any animal you liked, what would you choose to be?

In Summer When I Go to Bed

In summer when I go to bed
The sun still streaming overhead
My bed becomes so small and hot
With sheets and pillows in a knot,
And then I lie and try to see
The things I'd really like to be.

I think I'd be a glossy cat
A little plump, but not too fat.
I'd never touch a bird or mouse
I'm much too busy around the house.

Perhaps I'd be a crocodile
Within the marshes of the Nile
And paddle in the river bed
With dripping mud-caps on my head.

Or maybe next a mountain goat
With shaggy whiskers at my throat,
Leaping streams and jumping rocks
In stripy pink and purple socks.

But then before I really know
Just what I'd be or where I'd go
My bed becomes so wide and deep
And all my thoughts are fast asleep.

after Thomas Hood (extract from poem)

Reading

1. a) Why couldn't the poet go to sleep? b) What did he try to imagine?

2. How is the cat described?

3. Why do you think the crocodile might wear mud-caps on his head?

4. What is strange about the mountain goat?

5. a) How many verses are there?
    b) Write down any pairs of rhyming words you can find.

6. Read the poem on copymaster 20 and compare it with the poem opposite.

Writing

1. Here are two more verses from the poem.
    Copy them and fill in what you think the missing words might be.

    An Indian lion then I'd be   *I'd like to be a tall _____*
    And _____ about on my settee; *Making lots of people laugh,*
    I'd feed on nothing but _____ *I'd do a tap dance in the street*
    And spend all my day in my pyjamas. *With little bells upon my _____.*

2. Make up two lines of your own to finish off this verse.

    And then a snake with scales of gold
    Guarding hoards of wealth untold,

    _____

    _____

3. Think of two other animals you might like to be.
    Make up two more verses for the poem of your own.
    Write your ideas in rough first, and experiment
    with them until you are happy.
    Then write your best copy in your book.

4. Use copymaster 20 to help you write a poem called
    'Winter-time, Bed-time'.

In Praise of the Wind

Before you begin

The weather is very important to people all over the world.
How important is it to you?

In Praise of the Wind*

Trees with weak roots
I will strike, I the wind.
I will roar, I will whistle.

Houses not tightly roofed
I will destroy, I the wind.
I will roar, I will whistle.

Haycocks built today
I will scatter, I the wind.
I will roar, I will whistle.

The worthless slug-a-bed
I will wake, I the wind.
I will roar, I will whistle.

* The poem above is a traditional song of the Teleut people of Siberia.
Siberia is a very flat open country, where the wind is very powerful.

Reading

1. a) Where does the song come from?
   b) What do you know about that country?

2. What does 'to praise' mean?

3. Who do you think 'I' stands for in each verse?

4. a) How many lines are there in each verse? b) Do they rhyme?

5. What do you notice about the last two lines of each verse?

6. Read copymaster 21 for another poem from a different country.

Writing

1. Here are some more verses you could use in the poem.
   Copy them and complete them in your own words.

   Corn in the field   *Fire in the hearth*
   _____, *I the wind.*   _____
   I will roar; I will whistle.   _____

2. Make up some verses for a poem in praise of the sun following this pattern:

   > *Seeds under the ground*
   > *I will warm them, I the sun.*
   > *I will shine. I will glow.*

3. Read this poem from the Yoruba people of Africa.

   > *Enjoy the earth gently.*
   > *For if the earth is spoiled*
   > *It cannot be repaired.*
   > *Enjoy the earth gently.*

   - Write down some notes on why you think we should take care of our Earth.
   - (Copymaster 21 will also help you.)
   - Choose some of your ideas and turn them into a poem.
   - It does not have to rhyme.
   - Begin each new idea on a new line.

Memories of a Sweet Shop

Before you begin

Do we remember everything that happens to us?
What is your earliest memory?
What is your happiest memory?

Memories of a Sweet Shop

Yes, I remember that old shop well,
The two steps down and jangling bell,
The 'too high' counter and peppermint smell,
And tall jars all in a row.

Bull's-eyes, pear drops, sugar mice,
Honeycomb, sherbet and liquorice,
Aniseed balls at a modest price.
"How far will a halfpenny go?"

Oh, with what agony our choice was made,
And with what care each purchase weighed!
A three-cornered bag and a halfpenny paid,
In our childhood, long, long ago.

Anon.

Reading

1. What is the poem about?

2. How did the shopkeeper know when someone came in the shop?

3. How can you tell the memories are of the person as a small child?

4. Name some of the sweets the shop sold that were in the tall jars.

5. What clues are there in the poem that it is about memories of the past?

6. How can you tell that the person had difficulty knowing
    what sort of sweets to buy?

Writing

1. In rough, list down lots of your good memories (or you can make
    some up!)
    Choose some of the most interesting and write them down
    like a list poem.
    They do not have to rhyme – but they can if you wish.
    Do it like this:

    > *Some of my marvellous memories are:*
    > *learning to whistle,*
    > *seeing my new baby brother for the first time,*

2. Now do the same for some 'not so good' memories.

3. Copy and complete these two verses describing what memories are like.
    Add three more ideas of your own.

    > *Memories are like ghosts*
    > *Because they sometimes appear when you don't expect them to.*

    > *Memories are like hidden treasure*
    > *Because* _____

4. Use copymaster 22 to help you write a 'memory bank' poem.

The Digger's Song

Before you begin

If you use your imagination, lots of everyday things around us can come alive!
A pencil sharpener is a beast who devours wood shavings.
A lamp-post is a tall giant with one bright eye who sleeps during the day!
Read this modern poem about a mechanical digger and see what it has become.

The Digger's Song

I am a digger, a mechanical digger.
With my metal claws
I can scratch, I can scrape
Till I make the earth break.

I am a digger, a mechanical digger.
With my metal jaws
I can bite, I can tear,
Ripping holes anywhere.

I am a digger, a mechanical digger.
With my metal hands
I can scoop, I can lift.
Whole hills I can shift.

I am a digger, a mechanical digger.
With my metal teeth
I can snatch, I can seize
Chunks of earth, roots of trees.

I am a digger, a mechanical digger.
Where there's work to be done,
Send for me! I'm the one
Who shifts earth by the ton!

John Foster

Reading

1. What can the digger's claws do?

2. What can the digger's teeth do?

3. How many verses are there?

4. Write the pairs of rhyming words in the poem.

5. Which lines in each verse rhyme –
   the first two or the third and fourth lines?

6. How does the poet make you think the digger is alive?

Writing

1. Write your own descriptions of some everyday things in the home
   or at school. Here are two examples to give you some ideas.

   A hairdryer is like a buzzing bee,
   as it buzzes round my head,
   making me hot and bothered.

   A television is like a cyclops.
   It sleeps quietly in the corner,
   Then suddenly blinks and wakes up.

2. Copy and complete this poem about a vacuum cleaner.
   Add some lines of your own.

   > *My vacuum cleaner has a huge appetite.*
   > *It sucks up everything in _____.*
   > *Its long cable wriggles behind just liké a snake,*
   > *As the cleaner gobbles up crumbs of _____.*
   > *Its electric eye glows a yellow red*
   > *When it _____.*
   > *This hungry beast devours everything,*
   > *_____*

3. Make up your own poem about a machine on a building site
   (like a crane, a bulldozer, a tipper truck) that comes to life.

4. Use copymaster 23 to help you write a poem about Alfred the Robot.

A Visit from St Nicholas

Before you begin

What do you enjoy about Christmas?
Read part of a poem about Christmas written over a hundred years ago.
What differences can you spot?

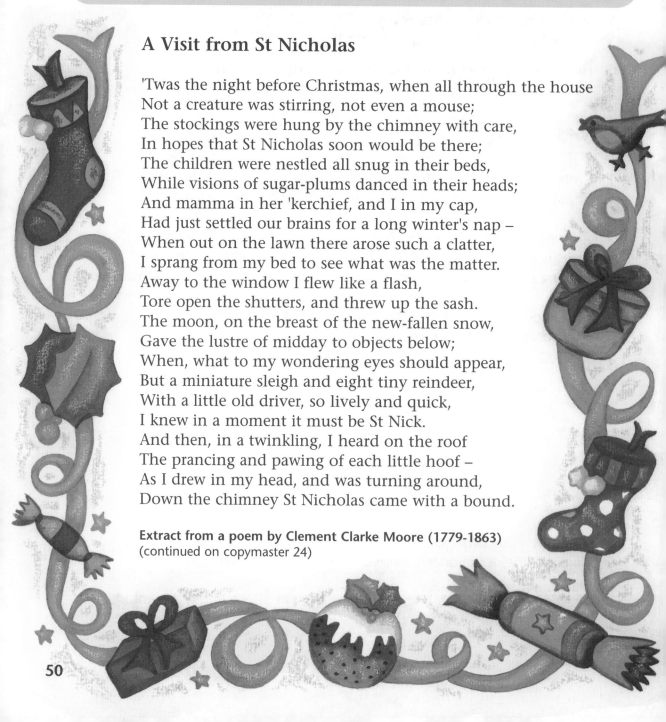

A Visit from St Nicholas

'Twas the night before Christmas, when all through the house
Not a creature was stirring, not even a mouse;
The stockings were hung by the chimney with care,
In hopes that St Nicholas soon would be there;
The children were nestled all snug in their beds,
While visions of sugar-plums danced in their heads;
And mamma in her 'kerchief, and I in my cap,
Had just settled our brains for a long winter's nap –
When out on the lawn there arose such a clatter,
I sprang from my bed to see what was the matter.
Away to the window I flew like a flash,
Tore open the shutters, and threw up the sash.
The moon, on the breast of the new-fallen snow,
Gave the lustre of midday to objects below;
When, what to my wondering eyes should appear,
But a miniature sleigh and eight tiny reindeer,
With a little old driver, so lively and quick,
I knew in a moment it must be St Nick.
And then, in a twinkling, I heard on the roof
The prancing and pawing of each little hoof –
As I drew in my head, and was turning around,
Down the chimney St Nicholas came with a bound.

Extract from a poem by Clement Clarke Moore (1779-1863)
(continued on copymaster 24)

Reading

1. Who do you think St Nicholas is?

2. Where did the children hang up their stockings?

3. How did St Nicholas enter the house?

4. Write down five pairs of rhyming words from the poem.

5. How can you tell the poem was written many years ago?
   Write down five old-fashioned words you can find in the poem,
   and say what you think they mean.

6. Read the rest of the poem on copymaster 24.

Writing

1. Make a long list of things you associate with Christmas.

2. Copy and complete the beginning of this Christmas counting poem.
   Use some of the things from your list to help you write some more lines.

   One St Nicholas all jolly and red.
   Two snowmen outside with hats on their _____.
   Three stars twinkling on the Christmas tree.
   Four cards on the mantelpiece from my friends to _____.

3. Copy and complete the poem below about Christmas.
   Make up two more verses of your own.

Christmas coming,	*Hands cold,*
Cold winds blow,	*Noses red,*
Icicles hanging,	*Central heating,*
Lots of snow.	*Nice warm _____.*
Christmas cards,	*Presents to wrap,*
Carols singing,	*Presents to buy,*
Decorations,	*I love Christmas –*
Church bells _____.	*I wonder _____!*

I Want to Be an Astronaut

Before you begin

Would you like to be an astronaut and explore outer space?
What sort of things would you do? see? hear?

I Want to Be an Astronaut

I want to be an astronaut
And shoot off into space;
I want to float like a silver bird
Above the human race.

I want to ride a rocket,
Computerised (with lights);
I want to go beyond the stars
I've seen on winter nights.

I want the Earth to watch me
On their TV screens;
I want them all to see me go
Amongst fantastic scenes.

I want to be an astronaut
And go to Saturn soon;
I want to step down on Mars
And the dark side of the Moon.

I want to spend my holidays
In a rocket that I'll fly;
I want to be an astronaut
Who waves our world goodbye.

I want to see the other worlds
And boys that aren't like me;
I want to see the strangest lands
And still be home for tea.

Peter Thabit Jones

Reading

1. How can you tell it is a child writing the poem?

2. List some of the places he wants to visit.

3. What does he want to float like?

4. What sort of rocket does he want to fly in?

5. Do you think the boy is just daydreaming? Give a reason for your answer.

6. What did you think of the poem?

Writing

1. Copy and complete some verses of your own for the poem.

   I want to be an astronaut
   And zoom off into space.
   I want to fly as fast as I can
   And _____.

   I want to be an astronaut
   And spend some time on Mars.
   I want to explore the universe
   And _____.

2. Make up and write two more verses in your own words.

3. Read these descriptions of the Earth and the Sun.

   The Earth is a blue-green beach ball,
   Spinning in pitch-black darkness,
   Lit up by thousands of twinkling stars.

   The Sun is a yellow yacht,
   Sailing serenely across
   A brilliant cobalt blue sea.

   > - Write your own three-line descriptions of each.
   > - Write your ideas down in rough, first.
   > - Keep experimenting and changing them until you are happy with them.
   > - Write your best copies in your book and illustrate them.

4. Make up some similar descriptions of the Moon and some of the planets in our solar system.

5. Use copymaster 25 to help you write about a space monster who came to town.

An Alphabet of Names

Before you begin

Can you think of a different person's name beginning with each letter of the alphabet?
The poem below will start you off!

An Alphabet of Names

A is for Arnold who loves drinking and eating,

B is for Beth who is always cheating.

C is for Carly who has lots of pets,

D is for Dan who loves making bets.

E is for Emma who always comes late,

F is for Frank who licks his plate.

G is for Gloria whose hair is in curls,

H is for Henry who can't stand girls.

I is for Ivan who plays football all day,

J is for Jade who makes things with clay.

K is for Kate who never washes her face,

L is for Leo – his writing's a disgrace!

M is for Mary who gobbles her food,

N is for Naomi who is ever so rude.

Reading

1. Why do you think these type of poems are called alphabet poems?

2. Whose name begins with: a) C?   b) E?   c) J?   d) N?

3. Who: a) is always cheating?   b) licks his plate?
       c) never washes her face?   d) has very bad writing?

4. Write all the pairs of rhyming words in the poem.

5. The poem is written in rhyming couplets. Explain what this means.

6. Read another alphabet poem on copymaster 26.

Writing

1. Work with a partner. Finish off the alphabet poem in your own words.
   Write your ideas in rough first.
   Make a best copy when you are happy with your ideas.

2. Write some alphabetical sentences about different jobs
   people do, like this:

   You could be an amusing actor or a bewildered builder.
   You could be a careful cook or a dangerous dentist.

3. Copy the beginning of this alphabet of food and drink.
   Finish it off in your own words.
   Work with a partner.

   A is for apples, so tasty to munch,
   B is for bananas, all in a bunch.
   C is for cake, with icing so white,
   D is for doughnuts, so soft to bite.

4. Write an alphabet poem of alphabetical verbs.
   Choose one of the following titles:
   'A Day at the Seaside', 'At a Party', 'A Visit to Town', 'The Football Match'.
   Here is the beginning of one to give you some ideas:

   A attempted to wind-surf.
   B built a sandcastle.

Toboggan

Before you begin

Do you know what a toboggan is?
Read the acrostic poem below about a toboggan and find out.
If you read the first letter of each line of the poem downwards you will see
that it spells the word.

Toboggan

Take me where the snow lies deep

On some hillside high and steep.

Boldly sit astride my sleigh.

One good push and I'm away.

Gaining speed now down the hill.

Getting faster – what a thrill!

At the bottom brush off snow.

Now! to the top for another go.

David Whitehead

Reading

1. Explain what an acrostic poem is.

2. Why do you think the poem opposite is set out so that it slopes?

3. Is this a rhyming or non-rhyming poem?

4. What other name does the poet use for toboggan?

5. Who wrote the poem?

6. Say something you enjoyed about the poem.

Writing

1. Compose an acrostic poem about yourself. Here is one that Alice wrote:

   Amazing, affectionate
   Lovely, likes lollies
   Intelligent, impossible to improve
   Collects combs and coral
   Enthusiastic, enjoys eating

2. Now compose one about SNOW.

3. Sometimes the word can be hidden in the poem, like this:

   Blowing
      litter
        in and out
          round and round

   Make up your own WIND acrostic.

4. Use copymaster 27 to help you write acrostics for FIRE, WATER and AIR.

Meet-on-the-Road

Read this conversation poem with a partner. Take different parts.

Meet-on-the-Road

"Now where are you going, child?"
Said Meet-on-the-Road.
"To school, sir, to school, sir,"
Said Child-as-she-stood.

"What have you got in your bag, child?"
Said Meet-on-the-Road.
"My dinner, sir, my dinner, sir,"
Said Child-as-she-stood.

"What have you got for your dinner, child?"
Said Meet-on-the-Road.
"Some brown bread and cheese, sir,"
Said Child-as-she-stood.

"Oh, then, give me some, right now,"
Said Meet-on-the-Road.
"I've little enough for myself, sir,"
Said Child-as-she-stood.

"What have you got that coat on for?"
Said Meet-on-the-Road.
"To keep the wind and chill from me, sir,"
Said Child-as-she-stood.

"I wish the wind would blow right through you,"
Said Meet-on-the-Road.
"Oh, what a wish, what a wish!"
Said Child-as-she-stood.

"What are those bells ringing for?"
Said Meet-on-the-Road.
"To ring bad spirits home again, sir,"
Said Child-as-she-stood.

"Oh then, I must be going, child!"
Said Meet-on-the-Road.
"So fare you well, fare you well, sir,"
Said Child-as-she-stood.

Reading

1. Who is the conversation between?

2. In which verse do you think the child realises
   Meet-on-the-Road is unusual?

3. How can you tell the child is polite?

4. What do you think Meet-on-the-Road looked like?

5. Why do you think the poem ended as it did?

6. Read a very different conversation poem on copymaster 28.

Writing

1. Think of someone or something you would not like to meet on the road.
   It could be:

   a robber   a giant   a monster   something else

   Think about what your Meet-on-the-Road looks like and
   what you might say to each other.
   Write a conversation poem like the one opposite.

2. Write a poem involving a conversation between one of the following:

   - a lady hanging out her washing and the wind
   - a child building a sandcastle and the sea
   - a footballer and a football

3. Write a nonsense conversation poem between two people.
   Always begin with a sensible question.
   Always give a nonsense answer, like the example below.

   > She asked, "What colour are your eyes?"
   > He replied, "Apple pies!"

4. Use copymaster 28 to write a poem called 'Irritating Sayings'.

Tall Buildings

Think of as many long, (or tall!) thin things as you can e.g. spaghetti, a giraffe's neck, a lamp-post, a worm etc.
Thin poems can be about anything.
Often they are about thin things like the poems below.
A thin poem makes a tall, thin shape, with only one or two words in a line.

Tall Buildings

Some
buildings
grow
so
tall
and
high
that
their
tops
reach
up into
the
sky.

A Piece of String

I
can not
untie
the
knot
in my
string.
My
piece
of
string
is a
knotty
thing!

Reading

1. What is special about a 'thin' poem?

2. Do the poems rhyme or not?

3. a) What do you notice about the words 'not' and 'knot' in the second poem?
   b) Can you think of any other homophones (words that sound alike) like these?

4. Use a thesaurus. Write down as many words as possible that have a similar meaning to 'thin'.

5. Which of the thin poems did you prefer? Say why.

6. Read some more thin poems on copymaster 29.

Writing

1. Copy and complete these rhyming couplets in your own words. Set them out as long thin poems.

   I have a trunk of which I'm fond.
   It helps me drink water from a _____.

   Spaghetti seems to get thinner and thinner
   but I still love it for my _____.

2. Copy and complete these rhyming couplets in your own words. Set them out as long thin poems.

   The long tall lamp-post lights my street
   _____.

   The baby sat in her high chair
   _____.

3. Make up, write and illustrate pairs of long thin poems about:
   a) a knife and fork   b) a needle and pin
   c) a pencil and pen   d) your arms and legs

4. Look at copymaster 29 and make up some thin poems of your own.

The Magic Box

Before you begin

If you could put some things which are very special to you in a magic box,
what would they be?
Read the list of magic things the poet thought of in the poem below.

The Magic Box

I will put into the box

the swish of a silk sari on a summer night,
fire from the nostrils of a Chinese dragon,
the tip of a tongue touching a tooth.

I will put into the box

a snowman with a rumbling belly,
a sip of the bluest water from Lake Lucerne,
a leaping spark from an electric fish.

I will put into the box

three violet wishes spoken in Gujerati,
the last joke of an ancient uncle
and the first smile of a baby.

I will put in the box

a fifth season and a black sun,
a cowboy on a broomstick
and a witch on a white horse.

My box is fashioned from ice and gold and steel,
with stars on the lid and secrets in the corners.
Its hinges are the toe joints
of dinosaurs.

I shall surf in my box
on the great high-rolling breakers of the wild Atlantic,
then wash ashore on a yellow beach
the colour of the sun.

Kit Wright

Reading

1. Why do you think the poem is called 'The Magic Box'?

2. Which is your favourite thing in the box?

3. Which of the things in the box are real and which are imaginary?

4. What do you think is the strangest thing put in the box?

5. Why do you think poems like these are sometimes called list poems?

6. What do you think makes this a poem? What is special about it?

Writing

1. Draw a chart like the one below.
   Make a list of at least four things in each column which are special for you.

special sights	special sounds	special tastes	special smells	things that are special to touch
the red sun just before it sets				

2. Choose two things from each column of your chart.
   Turn them into a list poem and set it out in verses, like this:

   > Into my magic box I would put …
   > the red sun just before it sets,
   > the dew sparkling on a spider's web.

3. Make a list of ten things you would love to buy at the supermarket and leave a line under each thing.
   Now add a comment about each thing on the next line, like this:

   > In my supermarket trolley I have …
   > a packet of crisps
   > to rustle in the bag and crunch in my mouth.

4. Use copymaster 30 to help you write another list poem.

Three steps to writing poetry

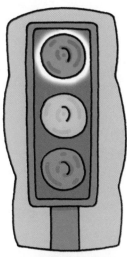

Ready

- Work with someone else if you can.
- Talk about your ideas together.
- Write down your ideas in rough.
- Don't worry too much about spelling or punctuation.

Steady

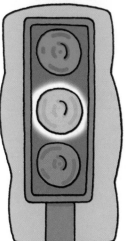

- Read what you have written.
- Talk about your ideas. Can you make them any better?
- Cross out any ideas you don't like.
- Add words you want to or take words out you don't like.
- Improve the words you have used.
- Try to use interesting, powerful or descriptive words.

Write

- Read your ideas again.
- Choose the best ideas for your poem.
- Check them for spelling mistakes.
- Check the punctuation.
- Think about the best way of setting out your ideas in your book (or on a computer).
- Make a best copy of your poem.
- Decorate or illustrate it to make it look good if you have time.